Responsive & Fast
Implementing High-Performance Responsive Design

Guy Podjarny

Beijing · Cambridge · Farnham · Köln · Sebastopol · Tokyo

Responsive & Fast

by Guy Podjarny

Published by O'Reilly Media, Inc., 1005 Gravenstein Highway North, Sebastopol, CA 95472.

O'Reilly books may be purchased for educational, business, or sales promotional use. Online editions are also available for most titles (*http://safaribooksonline.com*). For more information, contact our corporate/institutional sales department: 800-998-9938 or *corporate@oreilly.com*.

Editor: Brian Anderson   **Proofreader:** Kristen Brown
Production Editor: Kristen Brown   **Illustrator:** Rebecca Demarest

June 2014:   First Edition

Revision History for the First Edition:

2014-06-03:   First release

2014-07-30:   Second release

See *http://oreilly.com/catalog/errata.csp?isbn=9781491911617* for release details.

ISBN: 978-1-491-91161-7

[LSI]

Table of Contents

CHAPTER 1

Quick Introduction to RWD

Background

Mobile took the web by surprise. The fast growth of cellular devices (and subsequently feature phones) was impressive by itself, only to be compounded by subsequent disruptions such as the launch of the iPhone, the rapid and diverse growth of Android, and the emergence of tablets, led by the iPad. And the next wave of devices is already well on its way, with voice-based systems, smart watches, connected eyeglasses, and even connected mirrors and fridges.

As is often the case, many organizations initially chose to outsource the handling of this brave new world. Building in-house knowledge and technology is hard and time-consuming, and nobody knew for sure whether mobile devices were just a fad, or whether some new revolution would take over before the current one settled down. Even organizations that kept mobile internal usually created separate teams to handle it, separating this risky new turf from the more stable, revenue-generating desktop business.

For the mobile web, this separation manifested as separate mobile sites, known as *mdot* (or *m.*) sites. Organizationally, this separation was a good way to let independent teams work effectively. Technically, a separate mobile website was easier to tune for mobile displays and capabilities. Lastly, for many organizations, "mobile strategy" included both mobile web and native mobile apps, and mdot sites were aligned more closely with apps than with the desktop sites.

Dedicated Website Challenges

While useful, the dedicated website approach presents some significant challenges.

On the technical front, maintenance can become an issue. Maintaining two websites is not easy, and gets truly unpleasant when we start repeating the split for tablets, TVs, consoles, and more. Moreover, even within a category there is a huge range of display properties, input methods, browser capabilities, computation power, and other factors —making it impossible to treat all "smartphones," for instance, as one.

In addition, mobile device fragmentation and the fast pace at which new devices are introduced makes it hard to consistently identify a client device. Facebook is accessed by more than 7,000 device types every day,[1] a figure that is two years old and likely even bigger today. This introduces a need for dedicated device detection libraries, such as Akamai's Device Characterization, ScientiaMobile's WURFL, or DotMobi's DeviceAtlas, which constantly track and update the database of devices. In addition, even these dedicated libraries are limited to the information present in the HTTP request, which often does not hold some of the information we seek. For instance, while one could identify that a request came from an iPhone and determine the iOS version, nothing in the request indicates the actual model of the iPhone used.

On the business front, it became clear that users expect the mobile and non-mobile experiences to be completely aligned. The same user would often browse the same website through their laptop, phone, and tablet—possibly in a single session—and would expect consistent content, functionality, and style across all of them. The approach of "outsourcing mobile" is no longer viable: mobile has to be embedded into the core business and strategy.

Responsive Web Design 101

In May 2010, Ethan Marcotte proposed[2] an alternate approach to dealing with mobile browsing—*Responsive Web Design*.

---

1. *http://bit.ly/rf-fb-7000-devices*
2. *http://bit.ly/rf-RWD-alistapart*

Conceptually, Responsive Web Design (RWD) means having a single website that "responds" to the current device, and changes its design accordingly. The use of a single URL, also known as a *One Web*[3] approach, makes sharing links across devices easier, saves time by removing the need to redirect users from one domain to another, and is likely to improve search engine ranking because the single URL fits Google's "Dynamic Delivery" recommendation.[4] The adaptation means the web page would modify its design and interaction model to match the current device, striving to achieve an optimal user experience for a specific device.

To achieve this flexibility, Responsive Web Design relies on three primary building blocks:

1. Fluid Grids
2. Flexible Images
3. Media Queries

Implementing Fluid Grids means replacing any fixed size element on the page with a percentage, making its dimensions relative to its parent element and—eventually—the display size itself. For instance, instead of saying that the main content column is 512 px wide, say that it's 50% of its parent container. On a 1024x768 display, the resulting size will be the same, but on a smaller screen, the column will adapt to take up half the screen width, implicitly improving support for different display sizes.

Flexible Images is essentially the application of Fluid Grids to images, specifying their size as a percentage of their parent container. Note that this means the page needs to explicitly state the (relative) size of every image, using style rules for the image itself or a parent container. Responsive pages cannot rely on the actual dimensions of a downloaded image to determine how much space it will take on a page (a limitation that helps performance, as it avoids unnecessary reflows[5]).

Lastly, Media Queries[6] is a styling capability introduced with CSS3 to extend the simpler media types. These queries allow websites to set

---

3. *http://bit.ly/rf-no-mobile-web*
4. *http://bit.ly/rf-rwd-seo*
5. *http://bit.ly/rf-opt-rendering*
6. *http://bit.ly/rf-mq*

different style rules for different display properties (or any "media feature"). For instance, a three-column layout is common on desktop screens, but on a 320-pixel-wide smartphone screen, each column becomes too small to use. A Media Query triggers if the window is below (or above) a certain width, and overrides the styling to use a single column instead. The transition points specified by the Media Queries are known as breakpoints.

These three building blocks, when combined and well implemented, enable powerful web pages that seamlessly work on many devices and appear as though they were written exclusively for it. This helps battle device fragmentation, and even addresses devices that did not exist when the website was created, making RWD "Future Friendly."[7]

It's important to notice two properties that these three techniques share.

First, they're all client-side techniques, applied in the browser. This trait is expected, as RWD aims to eliminate the need for server-side device detection, replacing it with client-side feature detection (such as display size). Nevertheless, it has significant implications, as we'll soon see.

Secondly, all three techniques focus solely on styling. They dictate the way a page is displayed to a user and how users interact with it, but not the parsing and processing of a page, nor how its resources are downloaded. This property matches the problem RWD set out to address—the *design* of the page, not the underlying mechanisms.

What This Book Is NOT

Before we go any further, let's set some expectations.

This book is not a broad web performance book. Web performance is a big and complex topic, and there are many great web performance books out there, most notably Steve Souders' *High Performance Web Sites*.

This book focuses on the performance issues specifically related to RWD, and does not cover broader performance practices.

---

7. *http://bit.ly/rf-future-friendy*

This book is also not an end-to-end RWD book. While it covers some of the basic implementation concepts of RWD, it limits those to the ones that eventually impact web performance. Once again, there are many good books that can help you port your design, code, and entire organization to the world of RWD, and I would encourage you to read those.

Where this book fits is in the intersection between performance and Responsive Web Design, outlining the challenges RWD creates when trying to make pages fast, and helping you overcome them in the best way possible.

CHAPTER 2

Performance and Responsive Web Design

Responsive Web Design is a powerful tool, and is being rapidly adopted by many organizations. Based on my latest tests, roughly 11-12% of websites[1] are already responsive (or at least fluid). This quick and massive adoption is good news for users, as websites will become easier to use on mobile devices. However, it also means that the early implementations have not had time to mature and work out some core issues. More specifically, it means that implementations do not consider performance.

The Woes of Cellular

The impact of mobile extends far beyond design, and one other area it challenged is the world of web performance. For decades, we've witnessed a consistent and rapid improvement in our connection speeds. We've gone from slow dial-up modems, intermittently connected at 14,400 bits per second, to high-speed fiber connections reaching gigabit speeds. Akamai data shows that the average connection speed in the US grew 2.5 times in the last six years, reaching almost 10 Mbps in late 2013.[2] While many users still rely on slow connections to access the Internet, fixed connection speed is on a constant improvement streak.

---

1. *http://bit.ly/rf-rwd-ratio-2013*
2. *http://bit.ly/rf-akamai-soti*

Cellular connections, however, change this picture. While having connectivity everywhere is extremely powerful, cellular bandwidth is typically 3–4 times slower than fixed lines, often leading to poor experiences. Even worse, latency on cellular networks is often 10 times longer than fixed lines! Combined with congestion and packet loss concerns, cellular network performance often sets us back a decade or two in terms of providing a fast user experience.

Fortunately, mobile devices also use small displays, which naturally require designers to show more constraint. Smaller screens usually translate to fewer bells and whistles, and at times less content, both of which reduce the payload of the page. And indeed, looking at the top 5,000 websites, the mdot sites were more than 3 times smaller than their desktop counterparts.[3] It's possible this gap will shrink as mobile devices grow more powerful, but the smaller display will likely always force a higher level of scrutiny for adding content to a page.

Core Performance Problem: Over-Downloading

The limits of the small screen apply to responsive websites as well. And indeed, browsing a responsive website on a small screen usually means that less content is shown, images are smaller, and so on. However, when using Responsive Web Design, this reduction rarely translates to a reduced payload (see Figure 2-1).

As previously mentioned, responsive design relies on client-side technologies. This means the client has to *receive* the data before it can decide whether (or how) to display it. This is a fundamental limitation, as even the smartest browser cannot "undo" a download.

That said, most of the "responsive" instructions are embedded in HTML and CSS, which only account for a small portion of an average page's weight. This means that responsive HTML still has an opportunity to avoid downloading *some* of the resources it won't need. Unfortunately, this is where the second property of RWD comes into play —*responsive design deals in style, and style alone*. Media Queries and relative sizes can hide or shrink elements, but neither of those tactics prevent excess downloading of bytes.

---

3. *http://bit.ly/rf-resp-in-wild*

Figure 2-1. Small and big screen views of Boston Globe's home page; they show a different amount of content, yet both weigh roughly 1.4 MB

As a result, while responsive websites look like mobile-only websites on a smartphone, they often require a much bigger download to render. A recent mass study I ran showed that 63% of responsive websites were as heavy as a desktop site when loaded on a small screen,[4] despite the very different visual, and only 7% were half the size or less. Compared to mdot sites, responsive websites were 3 times bigger.[5]

This is not a theoretical problem—it's very real, and plagues the vast majority of responsive websites today.

Speed Matters

This bigger payload translates to a slower page load—potentially painfully slow on congested cellular networks. As study after study shows, such poor user experience quickly impacts the bottom line. A few examples include Etsy discovering that adding 160 KB of image bytes to their pages increased the bounce rate by 12%,[6] DoubleClick seeing a 12% click-through rate increase after eliminating a single redirect,[7]

4. *http://bit.ly/rf-small-vs-big-screen*
5. *http://bit.ly/rf-resp-in-wild*
6. *http://bit.ly/rf-etsy-perf-is-ux*
7. *http://bit.ly/rf-dblclick-ad-perf*

and eBay noticing a 5% decrease in purchases per week when the site was 35% slower[8] (reaffirming similar earlier stats from Walmart[9]).

Of course, Responsive Web Design also helps business outcomes by increasing conversions,[10] reducing costs, and improving SEO.[11] So how can we leverage responsive design without taking the performance hit?

Throughout the remainder of this book, we'll discuss this very question, describing the most common problems and offering tactical and strategic solutions for them. It's important to understand that the *concept* of Responsive Web Design does *not* conflict with a fast website, and that, with the right implementation, a website *can* be both Responsive and Fast.

---

8. *http://bit.ly/rf-ebay-perf-rev*

9. *http://bit.ly/rf-walmart-perf-rev*

10. *http://bit.ly/rf-lukew-rwd-impact*

11. *http://bit.ly/rf-rwd-seo*

CHAPTER 3

Image Over-Downloading

On an average website, the vast majority of bytes are image bytes. Regardless of responsiveness, images account for over 60% of an average page's bytes,[1] and over half of its requests,[2] far more than any other type of resource. This stat is true on mdot sites as well, with images accounting for roughly 57% of bytes on average (see Figure 3-1).

However, when comparing desktop and mobile, we see a different picture. An average mdot site requires less than half the image bytes of its desktop counterpart. This is an easy stat to fathom, since mobile screens are smaller, resulting in fewer and tinier images.

This reduced visual holds true for responsive websites as well. When the screen is smaller, there are often fewer images displayed, and those images that remain are smaller. However, in responsive websites we do not see the ensuing reduction in bytes. In fact, the average responsive website uses roughly the same amount of image bytes, regardless of screen size.[3]

This statistic, along with the large slice that images take of a page's weight, makes them a good place to start our over-downloading analysis. Looking across many responsive sites, we can see two recurring image-related performance issues in RWD implementations: "Download and Hide" and "Download and Shrink."

---

1. *http://bit.ly/rf-ha-bytes-per-page*
2. *http://bit.ly/rf-resp-site-made-of*
3. *http://bit.ly/rf-resp-site-made-of*

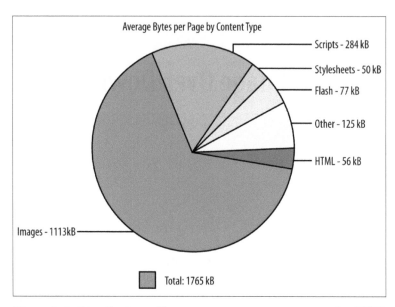

Figure 3-1. Distribution of bytes on an average page, per the HTTP Archive[4]

Problem: Download and Hide

When comparing the big and small screen versions of a responsive website, you'll often find that quite a few "big screen" images are no-where to be seen on the small screen. This feat is achieved using styling instructions. A CSS Media Query triggers when the screen is above or below some threshold, and in turn sets the display property of the image (or a parent element of it) to none or inline, indicating whether it should be shown. Various other styling techniques can also hide an image, such as setting the absolute position of an image to be negative (meaning it's "off screen"), or setting its width and height to zero.

In other words, on an mdot site, an image that isn't displayed is usually not even referenced in the HTML. On a responsive website, however, the corresponding <img> tag is likely to still be in the HTML and DOM (Document Object Model), but hidden using CSS. Unfortunately, hid-ing an image *does not prevent the browser from downloading it*. Re-gardless of the browser being used or the specific style used for hiding,

---

4. *http://bit.ly/rf-ha-bytes-per-page*

an image referenced by an `<img>` tag is almost guaranteed to be downloaded (Figure 3-2).

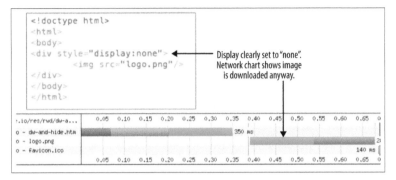

Figure 3-2. Image explicitly hidden using styles, but still downloaded

It's important to understand that this behavior is not a bug. Browsers intentionally separate the styling of a page from the processing of the HTML and the ensuing network activity, for various performance and maintainability reasons. In addition, CSS properties such as `display` and `position` are often used for dynamic interactions on a page, like a collapsible portion, an image carousel, or even a page area that is "swiped in." In such scenarios, the web page author *expects* the hidden components to be fully prepared, including the downloading of referenced resources, allowing them to be shown when desired with no delay.

This behavior, which we'll call "Download and Hide," is likely the single biggest driver of excess bytes fetched when loading a responsive website on a small screen. That said, being the biggest doesn't make it the only cause.

Problem: Download and Shrink

As mentioned earlier, one of RWD's building blocks is Flexible Images, which make adjusting an image to display size trivial: simply specify the image size as a percentage of its parent container. Using Fluid Grids, another core RWD tenant, the parent width also uses a percentage to state its size. This permeates all the way to the top, making all element—and image—sizes proportional to the display.

This approach works beautifully. The same page will show a `width:` `50%` image using 512x512 pixels on a 1024-pixel-wide tablet screen, while only using 160x160 pixels on a smartphone that is only 320 pixels wide. The problem, as you might have guessed, is performance.

Although the picture *looks* smaller on a smaller screen, the underlying image file isn't. The browser still downloads the full-size picture, as the same URL is shared across all displays. A 512x512 image includes more than 10 times the pixels that a 160x160 image does, meaning the small screen we mentioned does not leverage 90% of the data it received. See Figure 3-3.

We'll refer to this behavior as "Download and Shrink," as it's descriptive of the browser's actions. One calculation by Tim Kadlec[5] indicates that the big screen images are 4 times heavier than necessary on a small screen, and other studies show similar numbers. Remember that image bytes average over 60% of a the page's weight, implying that nearly half of the page's bytes may be unncessary.

Figure 3-3. Fluid image on Engadget shown using 35 times fewer pixels on small screen, but the same 55 KB file is always used

5. *http://bit.ly/rf-why-resp-imgs*

The performance impact of shrinking doesn't end with the excessive network. Once it reaches the client, a larger image means decoding more data, which may take 15-20 times longer than decoding a properly sized image.[6] After decoding, a bigger image requires the allocation of more memory to store it and subsequently more data passing to the GPU, at times through a slow memory-GPU connection (bus). Lastly, the GPU needs to spend more cycles to resize the image,[7] adding to the growing timeline.

Note that the same issues occur when using high density ("Retina") images. Retina is an Apple marketing term for a display with a 2x device pixel ratio (DPR), which means each CSS pixel takes up 4 (2x2) display pixels, creating an especially sharp view. Retina images, therefore, are in fact twice the width and height of a non-Retina image. When loaded on a non-Retina display, the Retina image is resized to fit its allotted space, incurring the same download and processing time penalties we just described.

High Density Images
While Apple's "Retina" displays use a 2x DPR, DPR is in fact a range; many devices use a 1.5x or as high as 3x DPR. Such displays, and the images tuned for them, are also often referred to as "Retina" or "High Density."

To summarize, "Download and Shrink" means we're downloading more bytes than necessary to display an image on a smaller screen, and subsequently overworking the client that needs to process them. This excess takes the biggest toll in an already bad performance scenario—an underpowered smartphone on a congested cellular network. In such scenarios, the excess alone can render a website unusable.

Solution: Responsive Images

The solution to both problems is often called *Responsive Images*. Using Responsive Images means loading images in a smarter fashion: avoiding the download of hidden images, and ensuring that devices with smaller screens download smaller images. Doing so will eliminate the

---

6. *http://bit.ly/rf-why-resp-imgs-part2*
7. *http://bit.ly/rf-css-gpu-cheatsheet*

"Download and Hide" and "Download and Shrink" problems, respectively.

Unfortunately, browsers do not currently offer native support for Responsive Images, leaving us with three possible paths: use CSS, wait for the browsers to improve, or use JavaScript.

CSS Responsive Images

I previously described how browsers consistently download hidden images, but in fact, that description is only correct for foreground images placed in a page using an `<img>` tag. Background images, on the other hand, go through a different process altogether.

Background images are added to a page using the `background-image` CSS property, which puts an image behind a DOM element. The DOM element does not have to contain other content, and so an empty element with a background image achieves a similar effect to an `<img>` tag.

Browsers process background images differently than they do `<img>` tags. While building the DOM, which contains the different elements on a page, the browser applies CSS styles to the DOM elements to construct a structure called the *render tree*.[8] The render tree holds the objects that will actually get painted on the screen, which means some DOM elements are not included in it (such as the page title, any script tag, or HTML comments). While building the render tree, when a node is determined to include a background image, the browser will download and render it.

For content elements on the page, the render tree usually resembles the DOM, but the two are not exactly the same. For example, a `hover` style on a DOM element may be represented as a child node in the render tree alone. On the flip side, when a node is marked as `display:none`, it is removed from the render tree (along with its children), and thus background images on its child nodes will not be seen or downloaded.

Furthermore, since background images are set using a style, they can be set within a Media Query condition. Using Media Queries, we can

---

8. *http://bit.ly/rf-how-browsers-work*

set different background images for different displays, and address the "Download and Shrink" problem as well.

Responsive Background Image Pitfalls

At first glance, using CSS as a vehicle for Responsive Images looks promising. However, a closer inspection reveals many reasons not to do so.

One such reason is that responsive background images are still prone to excessive downloads. For instance, the background image of a hidden element *is* downloaded unless a *parent element* is hidden. Even worse, when CSS sets one background image and then overrides it with another within a Media Query, many browsers will download both images,[9] despite displaying only one. These are symptoms of the fact that background image processing—specifically how it interacts with the render tree—is not standardized, making it very likely to differ between browsers and change over time.

To show one example, in the following CSS *banner.jpg* will be downloaded even on a small screen, despite being hidden:

```
<div id="banner"></div>
<style>
#test {
        background-image: url('banner.jpg')
}
@media all and (max-width: 600px) {
        #test { display:none }
}
</style>
```

In addition, using background images can get verbose. After adding multiple display properties, avoiding double downloading, and accounting for browser compatibility, a simple <img> tag can turn into a multiline mess. When you consider that the average page holds dozens of images, this verbosity can substantially hinder the readability of the page and increase its payload. This increased payload is probably more than offset by the savings in image bytes, making this option better than nothing, but it's still not ideal.

Lastly, beyond the syntax and verbosity issues, using background images as foreground images is conceptually wrong. Style is meant to remain separate from content (which includes foreground images),

---

9. *http://bit.ly/rf-mq-asset-download*

and mixing the two can create significant maintenance problems and confuse other systems. One such system is a screen reader, which is used to read pages out loud for users with disabilities. Such readers rely on the semantic understanding of the page, as well as alternate text tags like the `<img>` `alt` attribute. Using background images instead can make the screen reader misrepresent the page, and makes it harder to successfully provide alt text.

These are just three of several reasons not to use background images as your Responsive Images solution, but they're probably sufficient to demonstrate why using CSS background images as your responsive foreground images is not the best path.

Standardizing Responsive Images

If the two native image handlers in browsers—the `background-image` property and the `<img>` tag—don't give us what we need to make images responsive, why not enhance the browsers? And indeed, over the last couple of years, the W3C and WHATWG communities have been working through various proposals for new HTML and CSS tags that can support Responsive Images. While browser support is still minimal at best for all of these proposals, a few solutions appear to be headed toward broad implementation.

The Responsive Images Community Group
Want to follow or participate in the Responsive Images conversation? Join the Responsive Images Community Group (RICG)[10] to better understand Responsive Images, stay up to speed, and contribute in this space.

srcset

`srcset` is a new optional attribute for the `<img>` tag. Here's what `srcset` looks like:

```
<img src="banner.jpg" alt="Banner Ad"
     srcset="banner-HD.jpg 2x,
             banner-phone.jpg 100w,
             banner-phone-HD.jpg 100w 2x">
```

As you can see, `srcset` holds comma-separated image candidate strings, each holding a URL and one or more screen properties (for

10. *http://responsiveimages.org*

width and DPR). The browser uses the screen properties to determine which image should be loaded, and proceeds to download it. It offers a concise way to download smaller images to smaller or lower resolution screens, and coexists with the src attribute for backward compatibility.

It's important to note that srcset is considered a *hint*, not a requirement. A mobile browser may decide, for instance, that since it's low on battery or it's on a metered network, it will download the low resolution image instead of the high resolution one. This effectively means that all the images specified in a srcset must hold the same content, since the browser may choose to use any one of them, which in turn means that you cannot use srcset for design purposes (known as "Art Direction").

Lack of support for Art Direction is not the only downside of srcset. Other complaints included its hard-to-understand microsyntax, the confusion created by using both width and DPR, and the high likelihood of requiring duplicate or overlapping entries. Despite all these limitations, the srcset attribute is still a powerful tool, and appealed to many browser implementers. It's already supported in Chrome (as of Chrome 34), has been implemented in WebKit (not yet supported in any WebKit-based browser), and is expected to be implemented in other browsers soon.

Responsive Images and Art Direction

While this book focuses purely on performance, Responsive Images are sometimes needed for design as well. The "Art Direction" use case for Responsive Images deals with loading different image *content* on different screens, matching the image content to the design. For example, text overlaid on an image may become unreadable when it's too small, and should change or be removed. Alternatively, a person's portrait may look too large on a big screen, and require some surrounding background to look good. Support for the "Art Direction" use case was a key reason the web design community championed support for the <picture> element.

<picture>

The next standardization effort, the <picture> element, attempts to address some of srcset's limitations. Here's one example of using <picture>:

```
<picture>
    <source media="(min-width: 45em)"
        srcset="large-1.jpg, large-2.jpg 2x">
    <source media="(min-width: 18em)"
        srcset="med-1.jpg, med-2.jpg 2x">
    <source srcset="small-1.jpg, small-2.jpg 2x">
    <img src="small-1.jpg" alt="A Puppy">
</picture>
```

At its core, <picture> holds one or more alternate image sources. Each source may hold a Media Query, for instance min-width: 45em, specifying when it can be used. Unlike srcset, this Media Query is not a hint; it's a requirement that browsers must adhere to, thus allowing web pages more control when needed (and specifically enabling the Art Direction use case). The srcset attribute is used for performance purposes, letting the client choose the image quality that matches its display, and a regular <img> tag is included for backward compatibility.

As you can see, the <picture> element is far more verbose and flexible than srcset. Its full spec actually supports additional capabilities, like support for image size variants or specific image types, as well as supporting such attributes directly in the <img> element. This flexibility makes supporting it in browsers more complex, and caused some doubt about whether it'll be implemented. However, by now it looks like browsers will adopt <picture>, and its development in several browsers is already underway.

Client Hints

While <picture> and srcset both use HTML markup, a different approach was proposed in the Client Hints[11] specification. Client Hints proposes optimizing images by using HTTP headers to perform *Content Negotiation*.

---

11. *http://bit.ly/rf-client-hints*

Content Negotiation is not a new concept. For example, browsers use the Accept-Encoding header to indicate that they support gzip, letting servers determine whether to serve back gzipped content or not. Similarly, browsers could communicate the width and DPR of a screen using an HTTP header, and the server could determine which image to send down.

Here's an example of an HTTP request that uses Client Hints:

```
GET /img.jpg HTTP/1.1
User-Agent: Some Browser
Accept: image/jpg
CH-DPR: 2.0
CH-RW: 160
```

Client Hints offers the same capabilities srcset does, including not supporting Art Direction (since older clients won't send hints at all, and browsers may choose to communicate lower values when low on battery or network capacity). Its primary added value is that it doesn't require changes to markup, making it easier to apply it to existing websites, and simplifying complex <picture> element cases. Since Responsive Images can be seen as a compression method of sorts, offloading its handling to the HTTP layer, as we do with gzip, has merit.

Standard Proposals and Hidden Images

Note that both srcset and Client Hints only help with the "Download and Shrink" problem, but don't offer a clean solution to prevent the downloading of hidden images. The image requests always get made, and while they're adjusted to the display size, that's still wasteful if the image is hidden.

At the moment, the <picture> element is the only standards proposal that addresses "Download and Hide," though some draft proposals from the world of web performance may eventually tackle it, such as "resource priorities"[12] and a potential <img> defer attribute.[13]

---

12. *http://bit.ly/rf-resource-priorities*
13. *http://bit.ly/rf-img-defer*

Responsive Images and Waiting for Layout

As we mentioned earlier, browsers generate a render tree alongside its DOM, to determine how to lay out and eventually paint the page. Creating this tree takes longer than creating the DOM, as it also requires discovering all the style rules (e.g., downloading all CSS files) and applying them. To avoid downloading hidden images, the browser has to wait for layout to complete, which can delay when images start being downloaded.

It's therefore best to only introduce this condition ("only download if visible") to images that aren't always needed. Let the critical images, which are always needed, be downloaded as simple images (albeit resized to the display size).

JavaScript Loader

While we work through this standardization process, we still need a solution that works today—and to achieve that, we're left with Java-Script. Using JavaScript for Responsive Images is fairly straightforward. Here's an example of how to avoid "Download and Hide" using a JavaScript image loader:

```
<script>
function loadReal(img) {
    if (img.display != "none") {
        img.onload = null;
        img.src = img.getAttribute("data-src");
    }
}
</script>
<img src="1px.gif" data-src="book.jpg"
     alt="A Book" onload="loadReal(this)">
```

In this example, the src attribute of the <img> tag points to a cacheable dummy 1x1 pixel GIF, which all images on the page would point to. The real image is mentioned in the data-src attribute, which is ignored by the browser. Once the 1x1 image loads (usually read very quickly from the memory cache), the element's onload event would fire, triggering our loadReal() JavaScript loading function. loadReal() simply tests whether the element is visible, and if so, copies data-src to the src attribute, making the browser load the real image. Since the loadReal() function may be called again once the real image is loaded, we also delete the onload event to avoid the infinite loop.

This flow means you can still use Media Queries to determine which elements (and images) to hide. Only the ones that remained visible would actually be downloaded.

Of course, real world implementations are rarely that simple. As we've seen in the standardization proposals, a full solution would need to do much more, like handling different images for different displays, offering backward compatibility for clients without JavaScript, and tracking viewport changes like a device flipping from portrait to landscape. Fortunately, there are multiple solutions available for this problem, so you don't have to write this JavaScript yourself.

One solution is to use a polyfill. Polyfills are JavaScript libraries that let you pretend that browsers support a newer standard they do not yet support. You can include the new srcset or <picture> syntax in your page, and the polyfill libraries would convert it to something the browser understands. Once browsers start supporting the standard, they will natively process the new tags; the library would do nothing in those cases.

There are multiple polyfills available today, the most well known being Scott Jehl's PictureFill.[14] You can find the latest ones by searching the Responsive Images Community Group (RICG) website[15] and mailing list.[16] Note that the HTML syntax the polyfills support may not be identical to the specs, due to browser limitations and the fact that the specs are not yet finalized.

If you'd like a simpler solution, you can use Imager.js,[17] released by BBC News engineering. Imager.js embeds the desired image dimensions in the URL, reducing the clutter in the HTML markup at the expense of flexibility. You'll need even fewer markup changes if you use the Client Hints polyfill,[18] which uses cookies to mimic the information Client Hints would send, allowing the server to adapt images without changing the URL.

Lastly, if you'd like to offload this concern altogether, you can use an automated front-end optimization tool (e.g., Google's mod_pagespeed

---

14. *http://bit.ly/rf-picturefill*
15. *http://responsiveimages.org*
16. *http://bit.ly/rf-resp-img-mail*
17. *http://bit.ly/rf-imager-js*
18. *http://bit.ly/rf-client-hints-polyfill*

or Akamai's Ion). Amongst other optimizations, these solutions will automatically modify your HTML to load the right image at the right time as well as generate those image variants, as we'll discuss in "Generating Responsive Images" on page 25.

Responsive Images and the Preloader

Constructing the DOM from the HTML is not simple, often requiring pauses while waiting for a script to run or for a CSS to complete downloading. To help speed things along, browsers use a second parser, called the "preloader," which parses the HTML without pausing. This parser predictively triggers DNS resolutions and resource downloads statically mentioned in the HTML that will likely be needed later on.

Loading images using JavaScript means that the preloader will not see these images, and they'll only be discovered when the DOM is constructed and the relevant scripts run. This is another reason to try to load your critical images using regular image tags, and is a strong motivation for standardizing how we handle Responsive Images in the future.

Choosing Responsive Image Breakpoints

So far we've focused only on how to make the browser choose and download the right image. However, this assumes that you've already generated the image, which has some complexities of its own.

First off, you need to choose how many images to generate. Per everything that was just said, a single image for all viewport sizes doesn't cut it, but creating a different image for every 1 pixel change in screen size doesn't feel right either. So the question is, how many image variants do we need?

Since we're dealing with the performance aspect alone, the answer lies in the file size difference across image variants. For small images, like a logo or an icon, a single image for all viewports is probably good enough, since chances are the image would be delivered in a single roundtrip to the browser even at its full size. For very large and complex images, it may be worthwhile to have 10 different versions, as each step-down in file size may shave dozens of kilobytes. If you want to go the distance, you can choose the number of variants separately per image,[19] trying to meet a predefined performance budget.[20]

Generating such image-specific breakpoints, however, is an effort not everybody wants to undertake. While less optimal, it's easier to maintain the same image size breakpoints across the entire site than have custom ones per image. If you choose this path, I'd suggest a minimum of two screen sizes (aimed at smartphone and tablet/desktop), each with a regular and a high-density (Retina) version.

Generating Responsive Images

So by now, you've chosen the number of variants you want and the way to make the browser choose the right variant at the right time. All you need to do is actually generate these image variants.

If your site is small or light on images, you can probably generate the image variants manually during the creative process, and store them using a reasonable naming convention, like *banner-smartphone.jpg* or *banner-320px.jpg*. If your site is a bit bigger or updates images more frequently, you can automate the variant generation using tools like ImageMagick, and again store the variants with consistent naming.

These approaches work well, but they tend to break as websites scale. If you have 100,000 products in a catalog, have 5 images of each, and now need to generate even 4 variants of each, you're going to need some serious computing power, as well as a place to store 2 million images. Even worse, whenever a design change or a popular new device type requires a new breakpoint, you'll need to go back and regenerate all of your images.

A more scalable approach is to use an image transcoding service. These are online services that transform images on the fly, according to parameters embedded into the URL. In other words, your client-side code can determine the image properties it desires and simply embed them into the URL, and the service will generate the image in real time. When combined with Client Hints or a similar polyfill, image transcoding services can even act on these hints instead of query parameters, removing the need to modify the URL.

---

19. *http://bit.ly/rf-resp-img-jumps*
20. *http://bit.ly/rf-perf-budget*

For example, to resize a banner image to 400:320 using the Akamai Image Converter,[21] you'd specify a `resize=400:320` query parameter in your image request (routed through Akamai), resulting in a URL that looks something like this:

```
http://www.website.com/banner.png?resize=400:320
```

If you're looking for a free tool to achieve a similar result, and don't mind some loss of control, you can use Sencha.io Src for a URL that looks like this:

```
http://src.sencha.io/400/320/http://sencha.com/files/u.jpg
```

Of course, you can also create your own DIY image transcoding service, such as BBC News did with their Image Chef[22] tool. Such DIY services usually use ImageMagick or similar tools behind the scenes, and you may be able to justify the investment for large-scale websites.

Image transcoding services are growing in popularity as the need for more complex image handling increases. In addition to simplifying Responsive Images, they usually offer a variety of other image manipulations, and are a good way to support browser-specific image formats like WebP and JPEG XR.

Summarizing Responsive Images

Excessive image bytes are the primary cause for slowing down responsive websites. Downloading hidden and oversized images can easily double (or more) the payload of a page, without any added value. Therefore, if you choose to do only one thing to help RWD performance, it should be to implement Responsive Images. Today, your best bet for implementing Responsive Images is probably combining a JavaScript image loader with an image transcoding service, though the various other options mentioned in this chapter are good alternatives.

That said, while image over-downloading is the primary RWD performance pain point, it's not the only one, as we'll see in the next chapters.

---

21. *http://bit.ly/rf-akamai-ic-demo*

22. *http://bit.ly/rf-image-chef*

CHAPTER 4

JavaScript and CSS Over-Downloading

HTML references three primary types of resources: images, JavaScript, and CSS. While images account for the bulk of page bytes, CSS and JavaScript do carry their own weight, adding up to roughly 20% of page bytes. If we compare RWD sites to mdot sites, we can see that the number of requests and bytes required by an average RWD website is more than double those that an mdot site uses (Figure 4-1). Therefore, if we cut the JavaScript and CSS payload on a responsive site to mdot levels, we would reduce page weight by roughly 10%!

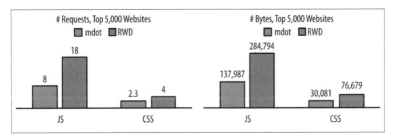

Figure 4-1. An average RWD website requires far more JavaScript and CSS requests and bytes than its mdot counterpart

While shaving 10% of the page bytes is a worthy goal by itself, the value of such an optimization does not end there.

CSS and JavaScript Rendering Impact

Downloading an image, while not always simple, is a fairly well contained task for a browser. Since images are static, the browser can download and process many of them in parallel, without worrying about how they'll interact with each other or with the rest of the page. Browsers do need to prioritize when and how many images are downloaded, as they handle content for network and compute cycles, but otherwise image resources are fairly autonomous. Processing CSS and JavaScript, in contrast, is far more involved.

When downloading CSS, browsers go to great lengths to avoid showing the user an unstyled page. As a result, most browsers will keep a page blank until all the CSS has been downloaded and processed, and the page can be accurately laid out. This means that getting the CSS becomes one of the most important steps in rendering a page quickly; as a result, browsers often block the downloading of other resources (primarily images) until all CSS files have been fetched. Walking the line between downloading resources in parallel and prioritizing CSS downloads is a difficult task, one that is handled differently by different browsers.

Downloading and processing JavaScript is no less complex, since any script can dynamically change a page in hugely impactful ways. For instance, scripts can inject content directly into the HTML parser, using a method called `document.write()`, possibly adding brand new sections to a page or commenting portions out. Other scripts may not manipulate the page, but set critical cookies that will be required by resources later on, or even navigate away from the page. Note that scripts *can* be marked as `async`, thus reducing their impact on the page load. Making scripts `async` is definitely the right way to go, but since doing so limits the script and interferes with execution order, it's not always an option.

Since browsers cannot anticipate what a script will do, each script tag forces them to pause, download, and execute the external script, and only then continue. Note that each such pause means a delay in the rendering of the page as well—which means that every script tag blocks the rendering of everything that follows it in the HTML. While browsers do attempt to predictively download scripts ahead of time, the fact remains that a script's impact on a page's load time far outweighs its size.

Given the page-wide impact CSS and JavaScript files have on a page's load, over-downloading such resources can have a massive impact on web page performance, far beyond the sheer number of bytes.

Problem: Hidden Single Point Of Failure (SPOF)

Another way in which JavaScript can affect page performance is by introducing risk. Consider a responsive website with a top ad banner. The site is simple—show an ad at the top, and the news below it. Here's a snippet of its HTML:

```html
<html>
    <head><title>Gadget News</title></head>
<body>
    <!-- Hide banner ad on small screens -->
    <style>
    @media (max-width: 480px) {
        #ad {display:none}
    }
    </style>

    <!-- Display ad -->
    <div id="ad">
        <script src="//awesomeads.com/banner.js"></script>
    </div>
    <!-- The actual news -->
    <div id="news">...</div>
</body>
</html>
```

Like most ads, the ad is added to the page as a synchronous script. As we've just explained, this means that it blocks the rendering of all the content below it—nothing will be displayed until the ad script is downloaded and executed. This may not be a big issue most of the time, but if the third-party ad service is having issues, the page may remain blank for a very long time, effectively making the entire "Gadget News" website unavailable. This performance and reliability issue is often referred to as *Single Point of Failure* (SPOF), as each third-party ad integrated in this manner is able to singlehandedly fail a site.

While unfortunate, this is a common pattern for a variety of reasons. Sometimes the ad network makes use of the document.write() method mentioned above, and does not support async scripts. Other times, the business believes that rendering the ads as quickly as possible is the most important step, since that's how the website makes money.

And other times, of course, it's simply because the first or third party didn't appreciate the risk or were not willing to make the effort to address it.

Consider, however, what happens when this HTML is loaded on a small screen. Using a Media Query, the ad is hidden from the user. This is again a common occurrence, as having less screen real estate pressures the mobile view to eliminate page parts that aren't the core content. Elements such as ads, social streams, product reviews, and live chat buttons are often removed.

In this case, however, the ad wasn't *actually* removed. Instead, it was hidden. And as we've mentioned before, hiding a script doesn't make it go away. The script will still be downloaded and executed (and likely even create the actual ad), despite the fact that it's hidden all along. The hidden script will still slow down rendering—at best delaying it and at worst, if the ad service froze, effectively taking the first-party site down.

Having a SPOF is not great, but having a hidden SPOF is simply wasteful. There's nothing to be gained from having the script on the page in the first place, and you would likely not include it at all in a mobile-only site. As we've seen before, an average RWD site uses 10 more JavaScript files than its mdot counterpart. Many of these files are unnecessary, and each one adds another slight delay and an unnecessary failure point to the page.

Solution: Conditional Loading

Since excess CSS and JavaScript can slow down a site or make it less reliable, we should look for a way to only download the resources we actually need. Unfortunately, as we've seen with images, there's no native way to keep browsers from downloading JavaScript and CSS resources not needed for this viewport. And as with images, the only way to truly avoid the extra download in today's browser is with Java-Script.

Loading the right resource using JavaScript is usually referred to as *conditional loading*. Conditional loading is a simple concept: instead of including a JavaScript or CSS link on the page, have JavaScript add it *only if necessary*. A very simple conditional loader might look like this:

```
<script>
if (document.documentElement.clientWidth > 640) {
    document.write(
        '<script src="//ads.com/banner.js"><\/script>');
    document.write(
        '<script src="livechat.js"><\/script>');
}
</script>
```

The script simply queries the screen width, and adds the banner and livechat scripts only if the screen is large enough. On a small screen, the script will never be added, and thus never be downloaded nor executed. While extremely simple, this code would actually work quite well as-is. That said, there are several ways in which it can be improved:

- Replace the `document.write()` method by inserting an `async` script element into the DOM (can only be applied to scripts that support running asynchronously).

- Use the `matchMedia()` method to define the breakpoint using CSS Media Queries; this is a more standard way of defining such markers and supports using other breakpoint markers, such as ems.[1] Be sure to use the matchMedia.js polyfill[2] for older browsers.

- Move the condition to be a `data-` attribute on the relevant tag, making it easier to maintain.

Applying all three modifications (but sticking to pixel units) results in something like this:

```
<script data-mq="(min-width: 640px)"
    data-src="//ads.com/banner.js"></script>
<script data-mq="(min-width: 640px)"
    data-src="livechat.js" ></script>
<script>
var scripts = document.getElementsByTagName("script");
for(var i=0;i<scripts.length; i++)
{
    // Test if the Media Query matches
    var mq = scripts[i].getAttribute("data-mq");
    if (mq && window.matchMedia(mq).matches)
    {
        // If so, append the new (async) element.
        var s = document.createElement("script");
        s.type = 'text/javascript';
```

1. *http://bit.ly/rf-ems*
2. *http://bit.ly/rf-match-media-polyfill*

```
                    s.src = scripts[i].getAttribute("data-src");
                    document.body.appendChild(s);
            }
      }
      </script>
```

This code implements all three changes, but each change can be applied independently as well. In addition, the same flow can be applied to CSS link elements[3] by changing the filter to find relevant link elements, and changing the attribute to `href`. Lastly, browsers without JavaScript can be supported using `<noscript>` tags.

Note that this type of conditional loading does have a a couple of limitations.

First, it interferes with the preloader, just like a JavaScript-based image loader would. You'll be well served to place all the relevant script elements in one script, as this will let the browser see them all together, and so download them in the best way it can. Note that scripts that require a specific place in the page may need to be added separately, and possibly use `document.write()`.

Second, it's hard to maintain script execution order when loading scripts dynamically. Where possible, I would suggest combining any scripts that need to run in order into a single file, and loading it asynchronously. You can also use the `onload` event of the script tag to call a specific inline function. The function will be called after the external script was downloaded and executed, allowing for some ordering even with `async` scripts.

Even with those limitations, conditional loading is a relatively easy way to eliminate many of the unnecessary delays and additional risks on a responsive site, caused by excess JavaScript and CSS.

Including Multi-Viewport CSS

Since much of RWD's secret sauce lies in styling rules, it's not surprising to see that responsive sites use more CSS files and bytes than even an average desktop website. This CSS holds the styling rules for multiple viewports, which are—by definition—more than the minimum necessary for the current viewport.

---

3. *http://bit.ly/rf-mq-cond-loading*

These additional rules can be included in three not-mutually-exclusive ways:

- A single CSS file with multiple Media Queries within it
- Separate CSS files with a Media Query in the `link` tag that includes them
- Inline style tags with Media Queries

The most common practice is the first: use a small number of files (usually split by page areas), and within each, specify Media Queries to adapt to the display. For example, a *menu.css* file may hold the styles for all the different ways a menu may be displayed as screen size changes. This approach is often developer/designer friendly, but it carries with it a performance penalty. Since the Media Queries are inside the CSS file, the browser has no choice but to download and parse the entire file before ignoring the unmatched Media Queries.

The second approach, while less popular, performs better, since it informs the browser of the Media Query each CSS file applies to *before downloading the file*. Most browsers will still download this CSS file (for various reasons,[4] some better than others), but will likely defer the download to the end of the page to keep such files from blocking rendering. Using conditional loading, as mentioned above, can eliminate the download completely.

The Build System: Your Friend

The way you code your files does not have to be the way you deliver them. Your build system is likely already packaging your code into a more deployment-friendly format. As part of the same process, you can easily convert files from a developer-friendly format to a more efficient one, with optimizations ranging from minification to separating out Media Query-specific files.

Lastly, the third approach, inlining the style rules, is not very commonly used. Inlining is a good page acceleration technique for first-time visitors, but it gets in the way of caching the CSS files, slowing down the subsequent page views. While powerful, inlining should only

---

4. *http://bit.ly/rf-mob-design-implications*

be used for very small objects or for content that is critical to the page load. Unless your systems are able to inline only the critical content for this viewport, or are using automated front-end optimization tools to do so for you (e.g., Akamai's Ion or Google's mod_pagespeed), I would not recommend inlining your CSS.

Summarizing Responsive JavaScript and CSS

Over-downloading of JavaScript and CSS impacts the user experience far more than what the byte reduction implies. To avoid over-downloading and maximize reliability, I would suggest that you:

- *Make as many scripts asynchronous as you can*; this makes it easier to conditionally load and imposes less risk on the page.

- *Split your CSS files by breakpoint,* and include Media Queries on the link tag itself to inform the browser when to use them.

- *Use conditional loading to avoid excess downloads,* as even async scripts and media-tagged links would be downloaded, costing time and bandwidth.

CHAPTER 5

HTML Over-Downloading

By now we've covered the three primary resource types, leaving us with one primary gap—the HTML itself. As we're used to seeing by now, the HTML of responsive websites is substantially bigger than that of mdot sites, averaging 41.2 KB for RWD versus 26.5 KB for mdot. While the ratio between these numbers is big, the numbers themselves are quite small compared to the overall page size. However, as the primary container for the entire page, the size and complexity of the HTML do impact the overall page performance.

DOM Bloat

As we mentioned before, browsers parse the HTML and construct the Document Object Model (DOM) from it. This DOM is essentially the page itself, and is therefore held completely in memory, supporting fast access and manipulation. Since the DOM itself does not care about styles (which are applied in the render tree), hidden parts of the DOM are still a part of it. These sections take time to parse and create, and consume memory as long as the page is loaded.

As an example, we'll look at the Smashing Magazine website's home page. This is a popular web development knowledge hub, and a well known responsive website. When we open *http://www.smashingma gazine.com* on a small screen, we'll see that 368 out of 652 elements are hidden—roughly 56% (Figure 5-1). If we look at the byte count, we'll again see that half the page's HTML is hidden: 43 KB of 85 KB. If this was a dedicated mobile website, it would likely remove those HTML fragments, saving half the DOM memory and complexity.

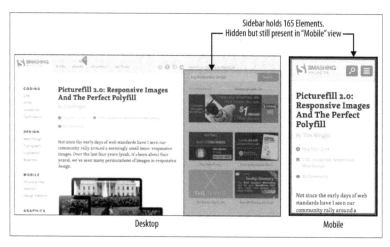

Figure 5-1. 56% of the elements on Smashing Magazine's home page are hidden on a small screen

Beyond memory, a big DOM also means that modifying the page would take longer. While some page changes can be done using styles (which doesn't impact the DOM), many dynamic page changes are done using DOM manipulations. A common flow for such a change would include searching for elements in the DOM and adding (or removing) parts around them, two actions that would be slowed down by wasteful hidden portions.

Conditionally Loading HTML

In the previous chapters, we saw that a JavaScript-based conditional loader can help us avoid excess download or processing. In all of those cases, the HTML was the container for the JavaScript code that performs such conditional loading—so how can we conditionally load the HTML itself?

While trickier, conditionally loading HTML is actually doable. Just as we've seen in the previous chapters, we can use JavaScript to add portions to the HTML only if the screen is the right size. Since HTML can contain many different types of tags, adding the HTML is most easily done using the document.write() method. This method, as we mentioned before, feeds content directly into the HTML parser, making the browser treat it practically the same way it would regular HTML content. Here's an example of a conditional HTML loader:

```
<div>Content That Always Shows</div>
<script>
if ( window.matchMedia("(min-width: 640px)") ) {
    document.write(
        '<div>A Long Section for Big Screen Only</div>');
}
</script>
```

While they work just fine, such scripts become cumbersome when the HTML portions get bigger and more complex—these are the cases where we care the most about not adding them to the DOM. In addition, the use of document.write() means the script cannot be made async, and thus will block rendering of later items. One way to address such issues is to include the HTML we'd like to conditionally enable in the page as an HTML comment, and then uncomment it if conditions are met. Here's a (slightly oversimplified) example of such a loader:

```
<div data-mq="(min-width: 640px)" class="mq-content">
    <!--
    <div>A Long section for Big Screen Only</div>
    -->
</div>
<script>
var tags = document.getElementsByClassName("mq-content");
for(var i=0;i<tags.length; i++)
{
    // Test if the Media Query matches
    var mq = tags[i].getAttribute("data-mq");
    if (mq && window.matchMedia(mq).matches)
    {
        // If so, convert all child content to HTML
        for(var j=0;j<tags[i].childNodes.length; j++)
            html += tags[i].childNodes[j].textContent;
        tags[i].innerHTML = html;
    }
}
</script>
```

This approach allows us to spread Media Queries throughout the page in a more maintainable fashion, and the loader script can be made async if included as an external script. That said, note that browsers process innerHTML (and similar methods) differently than static HTML (or content generated using document.write()), so certain elements won't work (for instance, scripts will not run). Be sure to test your content to confirm it works as expected when added dynamically.

Prioritizing Critical Resources

Over-downloading is not an RWD-only ailment. On most websites, any given page downloads a fair bit of JavaScript and CSS that it doesn't actually use. This gap is even bigger if you look at the content that is most critical to load, like the article on a news page (more specifically, the portion of it that is visible "above the fold").

The solutions we described to avoid excess content in RWD can also be used to defer the load of any content that is not critical. To do so, you could keep the critical content as regular HTML, while the rest of the content is commented and conditionally loaded as shown earlier. You can then invoke the conditional loading only when the original content finishes loading.

If you've already identified and prioritized the loading of critical content, you can even consider embedding the critical JavaScript and CSS into the page itself, a technique referred to as "inlining critical content."[1] Such inlining can get tricky, as different portions of the CSS may be deemed critical at different breakpoints, and so should be considered an advanced optimization—not your first step.

Summarizing Responsive HTML

HTML over-downloading has a cost in both network and local resource usage. Conditional loading of content helps, but still leaves some things to be desired. While it serves to reduce DOM bloat, and thus saves memory and processing time, the actual bytes of the additional HTML are still downloaded to all screens. In addition, on a bigger screen, the content generated with JavaScript is only discovered by the browser later (after the script runs), which may make the big-screen version of the page slower (and potentially more error-prone if we use the responsive comments approach).

To address these limitations, we need to move away from a purely client-side solution and introduce some server logic into our delivery flow, as we'll see in our next chapter.

---

1. *http://bit.ly/rf-opt-critical-path*

CHAPTER 6

RESS and Adaptive Delivery

At the beginning of this book, we described two mobile web strategies: dedicated websites (mdot) and Responsive Web Design. The mdot approach fell short when trying to handle the diversity of devices and sharing links between them, but did better in avoiding excess download. The RWD approach was better at adapting, but often resulted in bloat, hindering performance. Each approach has its pros and cons, which begs the question—is there a way to combine the best of both worlds?

Such an approach is referred to as RESS (REsponsive + Server Side components), a term coined by Luke Wrobleski.[1] It's a slight deviation from "pure" RWD, where the decisions were all made on the client side, but this deviation allows for substantial performance improvements.

Adaptive Delivery

Before we dig into RESS, we should mention a new and increasingly popular mobile strategy called *Adaptive Delivery*.

Adaptive Delivery means having dedicated websites, just like we did with the mdot approach, but serves all websites over the same URL. The use of a single URL alleviates some of the issues with dedicated websites, such as improving link sharing, removing redirects, and improving SEO. These benefits make it a compelling alternative to having separate dedicated sites.

---

1. *http://bit.ly/rf-lukew-ress*

Implementing Adaptive Delivery is often done by using a smart routing entity that sits at the front of your website's delivery, such as a CDN or a load balancer. The service determines the incoming client just like it did for dedicated websites, but instead of redirecting the client to a different website, it rewrites the forwarded URL to get the device-appropriate content (see Figure 6-1).

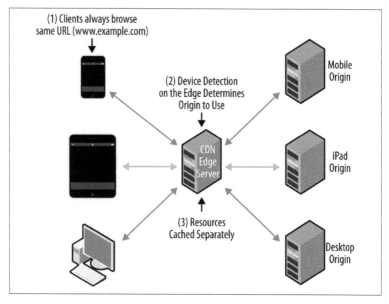

Figure 6-1. Adaptive Delivery using a CDN Edge; the Edge server receives requests, classifies the device type, and proceeds to the right origin, caching the results separately per device

While there's nothing responsive about it, implementing Adaptive Delivery is very similar to implementing RESS, and most of the information in this chapter applies to both.

Adaptive Delivery versus Responsive Web Design

Many organizations are deliberately moving to Adaptive Delivery. We mentioned its advantages over dedicated mobile websites, but there are also various reasons to prefer it over RWD.

One consideration is that it's often easier to go Adaptive than to go Responsive. Moving from a dedicated mobile website to Adaptive Delivery is quite simple, mostly requiring three changes:

1. Make sure your CDN routes users to the correct origin website.

2. Separate the cached responses returned to different devices (as explained in more detail later in this chapter).

3. Ensure that the same relative path (e.g., /news/) gets to the same content on all origin websites.

All of these are relatively easy steps. In comparison, switching to responsive design often requires more substantial rewrites to a page, taking more time and introducing more risk.

The second consideration, more relevant to this book, is performance. Like an mdot site, Adaptive Delivery benefits from the simplicity and lightweight nature of a website that holds only what a small screen needs. Like a responsive site, it doesn't suffer the slowdown penalty of being redirected to a different website. While there are many ways to make a website fast or slow, regardless of design, Adaptive Delivery makes it easier to be fast.

However, while fast and simple, Adaptive Delivery still suffers some of the pitfalls of dedicated sites. For instance, it almost always relies on user-agent detection to determine which client is accessing it, which can be error prone—it requires classifying devices into a single category (often hindering user experience on devices that are "in between" categories or screen sizes), and it doesn't handle client-side changes such as zooming in or rotating a device.

The ideal solution would be to combine Adaptive Delivery with a responsive client side, which gets us back to RESS.

Implementing RESS

RESS aims to deliver an HTML tuned to the current client, but always uses the same URL to deliver the page and keep the tuned HTML responsive, thus maintaining the flexibility of RWD. Implementing RESS requires making some decisions in three primary areas: content, granularity, and detection.

RESS may appear to be more complicated than the client-solutions we've mentioned so far, as it requires tooling to make decisions and changes on both the client and server side. However, for websites where the server-side tooling is flexible enough, implementing RESS may be the easiest path to a fast and responsive site.

RESS Content

RESS means serving different content to different clients. Therefore, the first decision you must make is which content needs to be served to which client. Since your server doesn't actually build a render tree, you will likely not be able to use CSS to make this decision. Instead, you'll need to duplicate this logic in the code that generates your HTML.

Duplicating isn't ideal, but it's also not the end of the world. Since we're dealing with a performance optimization here, there's no need to find every piece of HTML that may be hidden. Instead, focus on the areas that have a bigger performance impact, such as large portions of HTML or sections that include scripts and CSS that aren't always needed. This duplication will be an ongoing occurrence, and it's worth investing some time in deciding how to manage it (for instance, by storing the code of each component separately and pulling it into the page in real time using Server-[2] or Edge-Side Includes[3]).

RESS Granularity

Next, you must decide how specific you want your HTML to be. Conceptually, RESS can be used to tune the HTML to anything from a specific individual device to a broad category like "smartphones." In addition, it can use a variety of variables in its decision process, including display size, input type (e.g., if the device has a touchscreen or not), the existence of a camera, or the locale.

When deciding on granularity, we must again remember that this is a performance optimization. Many variables can be handled and tuned for the client in a more "traditional" responsive fashion, without any substantial increase in payload size. On the other hand, removing all

---

2. *http://bit.ly/rf-ssi*
3. *http://bit.ly/rf-esi*

the big screen content when loading your site on a smartphone is likely to yield substantial savings.

A decent starting point for granularity is the way we separate dedicated websites—smartphones versus larger screens. While simple, this initial separation quickly takes away a lot of the pain. Another good indicator is your site's use of breakpoints, as those are often opportunities to make more significant changes in how much content is being used.

RESS Detection

After you've decided how to divide devices and which content to serve to each, you need to actually determine which device is requesting the page right now—which means some flavor of device detection capability. This capability can be as simple as looking for the word "iPhone" in a User-Agent header, or as sophisticated as a detailed device database (e.g., Akamai's Device Characterization or ScientiaMobile's WURFL). Note that device detection is often just a prelude to *feature detection*, which translates the device to the features your granularity needs identified, such as the size of the screen.

To a limited extent, detection can also be done on the client side. A script, for example, can capture the device width and store it in a cookie, which will be sent with requests for future pages on this domain. In this case we're going straight to feature detection, removing the need to identify the device itself, which helps simplify things. However, client-side detection can only happen after the initial HTML was served and processed, meaning that the first page view will not be optimized. While not ideal, optimizing only subsequent pages or visits is better than not optimizing at all.

When discussing Responsive Images earlier in this book, we mentioned the Client Hints standard, which suggests adding request headers that hold the device width and pixel ratio. Such headers can also help the server generate optimized HTML for cases where display properties offer sufficient granularity. However, even under the Client Hints standard, the extra headers would only kick in when the website "opts in," again implying that the first page view will likely not be optimized.

As we'll discuss later in this chapter, the right detection tool for the job depends on a variety of factors, including the granularity you're looking to achieve, your budget, and the caching capabilities you'll need.

RESS for Resources

While we just discussed RESS as a way to optimize HTML, the same concept can be applied to serving resources. In fact, while we didn't name it RESS, we suggested this option when discussing image optimization, especially when using Client Hints or a similar polyfill. The server, made aware of the display properties through a cookie or header, can generate the correct image and send it down without a client-side image loader.

The considerations needed for tuning resources are quite similar to those needed for HTML. Decisions regarding content and granularity are still needed, and some detection is still required. Detection, however, is a bit easier when using RESS for resources, since we can use client-side feature detection and set the appropriate cookies or links in the HTML referencing the images.

While RESS can be used for any type of resource, it's rarely used for anything other than images. For CSS and JavaScript, the more common practice is to modify the HTML to omit or reference a different file as appropriate, instead of having the same URL return content.

Images, on the other hand, are very RESS-friendly. The content decision is simply the quality and dimensions of the image, and the granularity decision translates to thresholds. For instance, screens smaller than 480 pixels wide get an image that is 50% the original image's size, screens 480–960 pixels wide get resized to 75%, and the rest get the original image as-is. Since the granularity is a simple number that can be easily extracted with JavaScript, detection becomes simple as well.

Using a single RESS URL for an image has several advantages over modifying the URL to include the resolution, which resemble the arguments in favor of using RWD over a dedicated site. Here are the key ones:

Single URLs can be shared better.
    The image quality will be adjusted when a user loads it on a display with different properties, providing an optimal experience for that device.

Single URLs can be optimized beyond display.
    Image quality can be adjusted based on other parameters, such as the image formats the client supports (e.g., WebP on Chrome) or the network conditions (e.g., Akamai's Adaptive Image Compres-

sion[4]). A single URL makes it easy to combine all the variables and decide which image to serve, tuning the decision over time.

Single URLs are probably better for Image SEO.
While SEO always has a bit of voodoo in it, it's suspected that having the same image URL referenced everywhere will result in a higher rank for that one image than any split variant.

If you plan on using a single RESS image URL, it's critical to ensure that your Content Delivery Network (CDN) is able to cache it properly, which brings us to the next section.

RESS and Caching

While RESS offers great performance optimization opportunities, it also interferes with an existing performance optimization—caching. For the most part, caching services rely on the uniqueness of the URL, assuming that this "Uniform Resource Locator" indeed locates a unique and repeatable piece of content. This paradigm has been long broken for web pages, which have become very dynamic, but those pages were often not cacheable either. Applying RESS to cacheable pages and to static resources conflicts with caching much more often.

There are many cache layers within a single request path, many of which are affected by RESS. For the purpose of this discussion, we'll separate these caches into first-party and third-party caches. First-party caches are those are within the website's control, including the web server cache, load balancers, caching reverse proxies, and CDNs. Third-party caches are those outside the website's control, such as the browser cache, the ISP forward proxy cache, and corporate gateway caches.

First-Party Cache

Over time, certain first-party caching tools have evolved to allow caching at a greater granularity than a URL. This is usually done in one of two ways: caching based on the rewritten forward URL, or maintaining a dynamic cache key.

Rewriting URLs means translating an incoming URL to a different one, and then using the modified URL when accessing the next step

---

4. *http://bit.ly/rf-aqua-mobile*

in the page delivery chain. For example, you might use Apache's mod_rewrite to turn a product ID query parameter (e.g., *http://example.com/product.php?id=7*) into a path element (e.g., *http://example.com/product/7/*) for SEO purposes. Rewriting is an easy way to implement resource RESS—for instance, appending a cookie value to the outgoing filename (Figure 6-2).

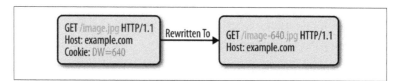

Figure 6-2. Example of an image URL rewrite, moving cookie value to filename

Once the URL is rewritten, all that's left to do is cache the resource based on the forwarded URL instead of the incoming one, making it unique again. For some applications, like Apache's mod_cache, using the forwarded URL is the default behavior. Rewriting is supported by many first-party caching tools, and is in fact the only way to handle RESS caching in most of those tools.

While rewriting the URL works well, some applications require the URL to remain unmodified, most commonly due to technical limitations of the application framework. For those cases, some caching tools support a custom cache key, usually composed of the URL and a variety of other variables. In such tools, the cache key can be made to hold the variables your granularity requires, read from a device library or an incoming header. Sample tools that support dynamic cache IDs are the Varnish caching proxy[5] and Akamai's Ion.[6]

A couple more points hold true regardless of the technique you choose:

Caching RESS requires changes to how you purge items from your cache.

Different purge actions will determine when a single variant is cleared and when all variants are.

5. *http://bit.ly/rf-varnish*
6. *http://bit.ly/rf-akamai-dpc-vid*

The cache must have access to the relevant detection variable values.
For instance, a device detection library at the origin server will
not enable caching by device within the CDN. The cache values
must be detected by the cache system itself (e.g., the CDN), or
communicated in the request earlier in the flow.

Third-Party Cache

Third-party caches generally cache by URLs and, since they are outside your control, the only way to instruct them is by using the standard
HTTP interface. In HTTP/1.1, and even in the imminent HTTP/2.0,
this translates to two HTTP response headers: Vary and Cache-
Control.

The Vary header instructs the cache to add a given request header to
its cache key. For instance, a server may choose to only gzip a response
for clients that support it, as indicated by their Accept-Encoding
header. Since it doesn't want downstream proxies to serve a com-
pressed response to a client that doesn't support it, it returns Vary:
Accept-Encoding with its response.

For RESS, the most relevant uses are to Vary by User-Agent, which is
the formal way an incoming device declares itself; and Cookie, often
used for custom identifiers. Unfortunately, User-Agent and Cookie
are probably the longest request headers, and each can hold an extremely large number of values—many more than the granularity we
actually want to split our content by.

This means the use of Vary for either header will likely create excessive
cache fragmentation (when every cache entry is applicable to a small
number of requests), and effectively disable third-party caches. In fact,
many caching proxies explicitly won't bother trying, and will simply
not cache responses that use Vary on Cookie or User-Agent. As a
result, the only practical value in using Vary: User-Agent is to indicate to search engines that your page may serve different content to
different clients.

The Cache-Control header guides downstream proxies on how to
cache a response, and supports separate instructions for shared proxies and clients. For instance, specifying Cache-Control: private tells
downstream cache proxies to avoid caching a RESS response, while
still allowing the client (for which we tuned the response) to cache it.

Given the `Vary` header limitations, the caching effect of `Cache-Control: private` and `Vary: User-Agent` is practically the same.

In summary, with today's technology, using RESS implies that the best we can do is disable downstream caching proxies. However, a new proposed standard, the `Key` header,[7] hopes to change this in the future. The `Key` header proposes a way to explicitly state the variables to include in a cache key, and do so in a standardized way. `Key` is not yet supported by any notable caching tool or service, but backing for it has been growing, which will hopefully lead to actual adoption.

Summarizing RESS and Adaptive Delivery

RESS and Adaptive Delivery are good ways to try to squeeze the best out of the worlds of Responsive Web Design and dedicated mdot sites. If your CDN or load balancers offer the right capabilities, it may also be an easier way to implement various responsive optimizations.

Keep in mind that RESS is a *performance optimization*, and you shouldn't think of it as an "all or nothing" proposition. It's OK to only optimize for the most popular clients. It's OK to only optimize the portions of your page that actually slow the page down. And it's OK to roll out RESS in a gradual manner, tackling the biggest issues first and working your way down the list.

7. *http://bit.ly/rf-key-header*

CHAPTER 7

Summary

Over the course of this book, we've outlined the different pieces that make up RWD's over-downloading performance problem, breaking them down by resource. For images, we've described how "Download and Hide" may result in too many image requests, and how "Download and Shrink" may cause downloads of oversized images. For JavaScript, we've seen how a hidden script may present reliability issues, and how your CSS structures may cause unecessary downloads. Lastly, we described how an over-large HTML response increases payload and—more importantly—the complexity of the site, making it easier to trigger additional performance traps.

Alongside those issues, we introduced increasingly larger scope solutions. We started from image-specific JavaScript loaders that help download only visible and properly sized images. Such loaders are really a specific implementation of conditional loading, which can also be used to avoid unnecessary JavaScript and CSS downloads. Lastly, we discussed serving device-optimized HTML using RESS or Adaptive Delivery, which can also be used to reference the exact resource files as an alternative to the smart client-side loaders.

All of these techniques boil down to avoiding excess download by either changing the returned HTML (RESS) or changing the resource loader (conditional loading), though implementation details may change from resource to resource.

What to Use When?

The right optimization to use depends on the specific situation. The current code base, size of team, tolerance of risk and CDN capabilities are just a few factors that can dictate which solutions can and cannot be used. That said, some solutions are right more often than others.

Here are a few guidelines that can work as decent defaults:

For images, use a client-side JavaScript loader.
> It's reasonably easy to do so, and will become even easier with the current standards effort. Resource RESS will not avoid downloading hidden images, and tuning every image tag in your HTML is hard, making a client-side JavaScript loader the right solution.

Prefer a single, cookie-based, RESS-enabled image URL.
> One URL is easier to share, can be optimized in many ways, and is better for image SEO. Use a cookie to store device width and pixel ratio (until we have Client Hints), and don't forget to add the cookie to your CDN's cache key.

Use a real-time image transcoding service.
> Device display size and resolutions will keep changing, and you will eventually want to adjust images to more than just screen properties. An image transcoding service, whether DIY or commercial, will give you this flexibility.

Use RESS or conditional loading for bunches of JavaScript and CSS files.
> Most of your JavaScript and CSS files likely appear near each other in the HTML, making it easy to cut them out of the HTML when needed. A RESS granularity of smartphones, tablets, and "other" is probably good enough to start.

Split your CSS files by breakpoint, and use inline Media Query.
> The irrelevant CSS files will be deferred and async'd when using a `link` tag with a Media Query, and it will spare you the complexity of loading CSS with JavaScript. If you have many breakpoints, merge the most similar ones to avoid CSS file fragmentation.

Use Media Query-based conditional loading for async JavaScript.
> For JavaScript files you didn't address with RESS, use JavaScript to conditionally add them to the page. Use Media Queries as your conditionals, to allow you greater flexibility and maintain your CSS syntax.

Use RESS for removing big chunks of HTML.
Losing the bulk of the complexity on a small screen will have an impact on weaker devices and worse networks, making this worthwhile. Focus on the larger chunks you'll remove—don't worry about small hidden fragments. If RESS is not an option, use HTML conditional loading instead.

The Bigger Performance Picture

This book highlighted the performance issues specifically related to Responsive Web Design. However, it's critical to remember that RWD is only a portion of the bigger performance picture. A responsive website may keep its requests and bytes very low across all displays, and be lightning fast even without addressing these specific concerns. At the same time, another responsive website may optimize for different resolutions, but still be slow due to a lack of CDN, unoptimized images, or blocked third-party scripts.

Tackling RWD performance can be an opportunity to develop a performance culture.[1] Actions such as introducing performance testing into your build process, communicating performance goals and celebrating their achievement, and running A/B tests to see the impact of performance on your business are all great ways to ensure your site becomes and remains fast, regardless of the technology you use.

Responsive and Fast

As we've seen throughout this book, while Responsive Web Design addresses many of today's usability and design challenges, it also introduces performance challenges. A standard implementation of an RWD site, focusing on content and usability, is likely to make mobile performance painful.

However, *Responsive does not mean Slow*. Each performance problem that responsive websites face can be addressed with the right implementation—and these implementations will become easier over time as standardization efforts bear fruit. Use this as an opportunity to adopt speed as part of your culture, and make the worthwhile effort to be both Responsive and Fast.

---

1. *http://bit.ly/rf-perf-culture*

About the Author

Guy Podjarny (Guypo) is a web performance researcher/evangelist and Akamai's Web CTO, focusing primarily on mobile and front-end performance. As a researcher, Guy frequently runs large scale tests, exploring performance in the real world and matching it to how browsers behave, and was one of the first to highlight the performance implications of Responsive Web Design.

Guy is also the author of Mobitest, a free mobile measurement tool, and contributes to various open source tools. Guy was previously the cofounder and CTO of blaze.io, acquired by Akamai in 2012.

A Note From Akamai

All of the author's proceeds from this book are being donated to Code Club.

Code Club is a non-profit organization that aims to give every child in the world the chance to learn to code, by providing project materials and a volunteer framework to support the running of after-school coding clubs. Learn more at *http://codeclubworld.org*.

Get even more for your money.

Join the O'Reilly Community, and register the O'Reilly books you own. It's free, and you'll get:

- $4.99 ebook upgrade offer
- 40% upgrade offer on O'Reilly print books
- Membership discounts on books and events
- Free lifetime updates to ebooks and videos
- Multiple ebook formats, DRM FREE
- Participation in the O'Reilly community
- Newsletters
- Account management
- 100% Satisfaction Guarantee

Signing up is easy:

1. Go to: oreilly.com/go/register
2. Create an O'Reilly login.
3. Provide your address.
4. Register your books.

Note: English-language books only

To order books online:
oreilly.com/store

For questions about products or an order:
orders@oreilly.com

To sign up to get topic-specific email announcements and/or news about upcoming books, conferences, special offers, and new technologies:
elists@oreilly.com

For technical questions about book content:
booktech@oreilly.com

To submit new book proposals to our editors:
proposals@oreilly.com

O'Reilly books are available in multiple DRM-free ebook formats. For more information:
oreilly.com/ebooks

O'REILLY®

Lightning Source UK Ltd.
Milton Keynes UK
UKHW022143250220
359325UK00005B/43